The Usborne
First Bible

The Usborne
First Bible

Retold by Heather Amery

Illustrated by Mandy Field and Maria Pearson
Designed by Andrea Slane and Laura Fearn
Edited by Gillian Doherty

The
Old Testament

The Old Testament

How God Made the World

Long, long ago, before the world began, there was nothing but darkness. Then God said, "Let there be light," and there was light. This was the very first day.

On the second day, God made the sky. Beneath the sky there was water everywhere. On the third day, he collected the water together to make seas. He put land between them and planted flowers and trees on the land.

On the fourth day, God made the sun to light up the day and the moon to shine at night. Then he put stars to twinkle in the night sky.

On the fifth and sixth days, God made everything that lives on the land, that flies in the sky and that swims in the sea, from tiny creepy-crawlies to enormous whales. Last of all, he made the first man and woman. He called them Adam and Eve.

On the seventh day, God had finished his work and he rested.

Adam and Eve

God made a beautiful garden, called the Garden of Eden, especially for Adam and Eve. They were very happy there, playing with the animals and eating fruit from the trees.

There was one special tree in the garden that God had warned them about. "You must not eat the fruit of that tree," he told them. "If you do, you will die."

One afternoon, a snake crept up to Eve and whispered in her ear, "Did God say you mustn't eat the fruit of the special tree in the garden?"

"Yes," said Eve. "He said that if we eat it we'll die."

"You won't die," said the snake slyly. "If you eat it, you'll be as wise as gods."

Eve looked greedily at the juicy fruit. "A little nibble won't matter," she thought. So she picked one and took a bite. "Try this," she called to Adam, and he ate some too.

That evening, God said to Adam, "Why have you tasted the fruit I told you not to eat?"

Adam hung his head in shame. "Eve gave it to me," he muttered.

"Because you have disobeyed me, you must leave my garden," God told them. "From now on, you will have to work to grow food. Things will hurt you and make you ill, and when you grow old you will die."

God watched as they walked slowly and sadly out of the garden. Then he sent angels with flaming swords to guard it, so they could never return.

Noah's Ark

Noah was a good man, who always did what God told him to do. One day, God said, "Noah, people have become very bad. I'm going to flood the world and drown them all. You must build an ark, a huge boat, and save your family and two of every kind of animal in the world."

Noah worked hard, chopping down trees and hauling and hammering with all his might. When the ark was finished, he loaded it with lots of food.

Just then, Noah heard a strange sound in the distance. Coming across the hills was a huge procession of creatures, all barking, singing, chattering, whistling and grunting. Noah watched as they crept, hopped, trotted, flew and slithered into the ark, two by two.

Noah looked up at the sky. It had become dark and threatening. Moments later, rain burst from the clouds. "Come on," Noah called to his family. "It's time to go." They all hurried inside the ark, and God closed the door behind them.

It rained for forty days and nights. Slowly, the water covered the ground. It kept on rising until it reached the tree tops. Eventually, even the highest mountains were underwater. Everyone was drowned in the flood – all except for Noah, his family and the animals in the ark.

For months and months, the ark floated about on the great new sea. Then the water began to go down. When Noah saw this, he opened a window and sent a raven to look for dry land. The raven found nothing but water all around.

Next, Noah sent out a dove. When it couldn't find anywhere to land, it flew back to the ark. A week later, he sent the dove again. This time, it came back with a leaf in its beak. Noah was very pleased. "This means that the flood is nearly over and things are growing again," he said.

But the third time Noah sent the dove, it didn't come back. Noah flung open the door of the ark. The sun was shining and the land was dry. He and his family rushed outside, and all the creatures crowded out after them. The flood was over at last.

Noah looked up and thanked God for saving them. In the sky there was a rainbow. "This is my sign," said God. "I promise I will never flood the whole world again."

The Tower of Babel

Noah's family grew and grew, and began to spread out. They all spoke the same language, so it was easy for them to live and work together.

They learned how to make bricks and how to build. Then some of them decided to build a tower. They set to work, piling up bricks and using tar to hold them together.

Higher and higher they built. They wanted to make a tower so tall that its top reached heaven. As the tower grew bigger and bigger, so did the people's ideas. They wanted to be famous.

God knew this would mean trouble. "This is only the beginning of what they will do," he said.

God decided to stop them before they went too far. He scattered the people to every part of the world. Then he mixed up their words so they all spoke different languages. No one could understand what anyone was saying any more. Never again would they be able to work easily together.

Abraham and Sarah

Abraham was a rich man who lived long ago in the city of Haran. He and his wife Sarah were very old and they often felt sad because they had no children.

One day, God said to Abraham, "I want you to go to the land of Canaan. There you will become the father of a great nation."

Abraham didn't understand, but he did what God told him to do. He set off with Sarah and his nephew Lot, taking their sheep, goats and everything they owned.

When they reached Canaan, they put up their tents.
There wasn't enough grass there to feed all their animals,
so Abraham and Lot decided to go their separate ways.

Lot chose the greenest land, where there was lots of food
and water for the animals, and Abraham and Sarah went to
the hills, where life was harder. Then God came to Abraham
and said, "How many stars can you see in the sky?"

Abraham began to count them, but he soon gave up.
"In time, your family will grow so big that you can't count
them either," God told him.

Abraham and Sarah grew older and older, and still they had no children.

One afternoon, Abraham was sitting in the shade of his tent when he saw three men coming across the hills. He got up and went to meet them. "Come to my tent," he said. "You can rest there and have a meal."

Sarah quickly made bread, and roasted meat on the fire. When the three men had eaten, one of them said, "God sent us here with a message. You are going to have a baby son."

Sarah laughed. "We're both much too old to have children," she said.

But Sarah did give birth to a son. She called him Isaac. Then Abraham remembered that God had told him he would be the father of a great nation, and he knew that God had kept his promise.

Rebecca and the Camels

By the time Isaac was grown up, Abraham was very old. He decided it was time to find a wife for his son, so he sent one of his servants to look for one. The servant took ten camels and set off for the city where Abraham's brother Nahor lived.

When the servant reached a well just outside the city, he stopped and prayed to God. "Please help me find a wife for Isaac," he said. "If I say to one of the girls, 'Please give me a drink from your water jar,' let her say, 'Yes, and I will give you water for your camels too.' Then I will know she is the one."

When the servant looked up, he saw a girl beside the well.
She was filling a jar with water. "Please may I have a sip?"
he asked. "Yes," replied the girl and she held out the jar. Then
she began to fill it up again, adding, "and I will give you water
for your camels too."

When she said this, the servant was delighted.
"Who are you?" he asked eagerly.

"My name is Rebecca and my grandfather is Nahor,"
she replied softly.

The servant went to see Rebecca's father and
explained why he had come. Her father agreed that
he could take her back with him. The next morning,
the servant loaded up the camels and he and Rebecca
set off together.

When Isaac saw them coming, he rushed to meet
them. He was very pleased when the servant told him
that Rebecca was going to be his wife. He fell in love
with her and, soon after, the two of them were married.

Jacob and Esau

Before long, Rebecca gave birth to twins. The first baby was pink and hairy. His name was Esau. The second was very quiet. His name was Jacob.

When the twins grew up, Esau became an excellent hunter, which pleased his father, whereas Jacob liked to stay at home with his mother. Isaac loved Esau, his eldest son, but Rebecca loved Jacob the best.

Many years later, when Isaac was old, he began to go blind. One day, he called Esau to him. "I am old and I may die soon," he said. "You are my special son. Go hunting and prepare me a fine feast. Then I will give you my blessing."

Rebecca heard all this and, while Esau was out hunting, she went to tell Jacob. "Bring me two young goats," she said. "I will prepare a fine meal for you to take to your father. Then he will bless you instead of your brother."

Jacob was worried that his father would be able to tell the difference, so Rebecca dressed Jacob in Esau's clothes and put pieces of goatskin on his hands and neck. Now he was as hairy as his brother.

When Jacob took the meal to his father, Isaac thought he recognized Jacob's voice, but when he touched his hands they were hairy like Esau's. "Are you really Esau?" he said.

"I am," replied Jacob.

Then Isaac fell for the trick and believed that Jacob was Esau. "God will treat you well and people will bow down to you," he promised him.

Esau was furious when he discovered that Jacob had taken his place. "You'd better go," Rebecca urged Jacob. "Your brother is so angry I'm afraid he will kill you."

Jacob walked for miles and miles.
When it grew dark, he lay down to sleep.
Soon, his head was filled with dreams.
He saw a ladder stretching all the way to
heaven, with shining angels gliding up and
down it. Then God spoke to Jacob. "I will
give the land you are lying on to you
and your children," he said.

Jacob stayed away for many, many
years. He married and had lots of children,
but still he longed to go home. He sent
messengers to Esau to make peace with
him and then set off for home.

When Jacob saw Esau with four
hundred men, he was afraid. But Esau ran
to meet his brother and gave him a hug.
They were friends again.

Joseph's Wonderful Coat

Jacob had twelve sons, but he loved Joseph most of all. He gave him a wonderful coat. Joseph's brothers were jealous, because they knew their father loved him best.

Then Joseph told his brothers about a dream he'd had. "We were in the fields tying bundles of corn and your bundles bowed down to mine," he said.

Joseph's brothers were very angry. "You think you're so much better than we are, don't you?" they yelled. They hated their brother more and more.

Another night, Joseph dreamed that the sun, the moon and eleven stars bowed down to him. Even Joseph's father was angry when he heard about this dream.

One morning, when Joseph's brothers were looking after the sheep, Jacob sent Joseph to look for them. When they saw him, one brother said, "Here comes the dreamer. Now's our chance. Let's kill him."

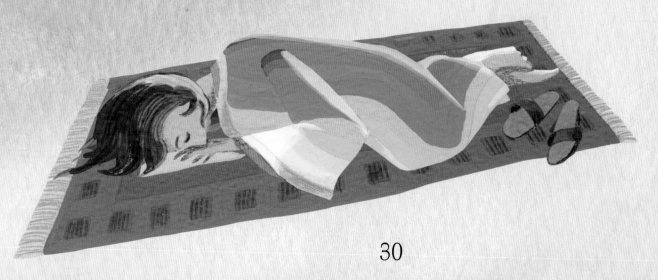

"No," said another. "We mustn't do that. Let's just leave him in that pit over there."

Just then, some merchants passed by. "I've got a better idea," said another. "We could sell him to those merchants."

So they did, but they kept Joseph's coat. They smeared it with the blood of a goat and took it to their father. "We found this," they said.

When Jacob saw the coat, he thought his beloved son had been killed by wild animals, and was terribly sad for a long, long time.

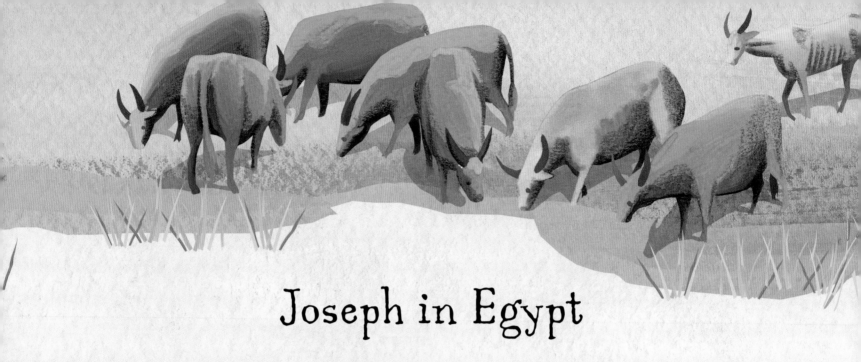

Joseph in Egypt

The merchants took Joseph to Egypt and sold him as a slave. Joseph worked hard, but one day his master's wife told her husband that Joseph had been very rude to her. It wasn't true, but he was angry and had Joseph put into prison.

While Joseph was in prison, the other prisoners discovered that he could tell them what their dreams meant. When he had been in prison for two years, the Egyptian king, who was known as the Pharaoh, had a strange dream. He saw seven fat cows on the banks of the River Nile, and then seven thin cows came up and ate the fat cows.

The Pharaoh asked all his wise men what the dream meant, but they couldn't tell him. Then one of his servants told him about Joseph.

Joseph was brought to the Pharaoh. He listened carefully and said, "Your dream means that for seven years there will be good harvests. Then there will be seven years of bad harvests, and everyone will be hungry."

The Pharaoh was so pleased with Joseph that he made him governor. In the seven years of good harvests, Joseph stored away all the extra food. When the seven years of bad harvests came, there was plenty of food for everyone.

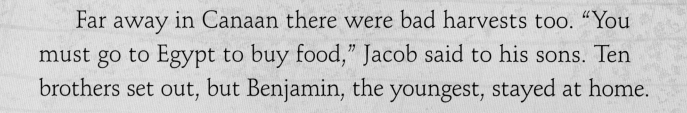

Far away in Canaan there were bad harvests too. "You must go to Egypt to buy food," Jacob said to his sons. Ten brothers set out, but Benjamin, the youngest, stayed at home.

When they reached Egypt, the brothers asked the governor if they could buy food. They didn't recognize their brother Joseph, but he knew who they were. He accused them of being spies and had them thrown into prison. After three days, he set them free. "Next time, bring your youngest brother," he ordered. "One of you must stay here to make sure you do."

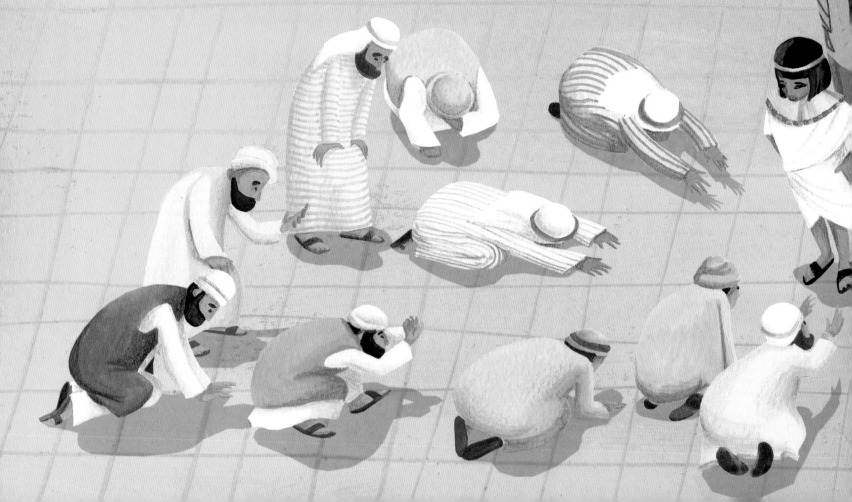

When the brothers returned to Egypt, they brought Benjamin with them. As they were leaving, with their sacks of food, Joseph's guards stopped them. In Benjamin's sack, they found a silver cup belonging to Joseph. Joseph had told his guards to put it there.

The guards marched the brothers back to Joseph. "You may go home to your father, but you must leave Benjamin here with me," he ordered.

The brothers begged him to let Benjamin go. "Our father has lost one son," they said. "If he loses Benjamin, it will break his heart. Let one of us stay in his place."

Joseph knew then that his brothers had changed. "It's me, Joseph," he said and hugged them. "It was God's plan that I should come to Egypt and save you from starving," he said. "Go back to my father and bring him here, and we'll all live together in Egypt."

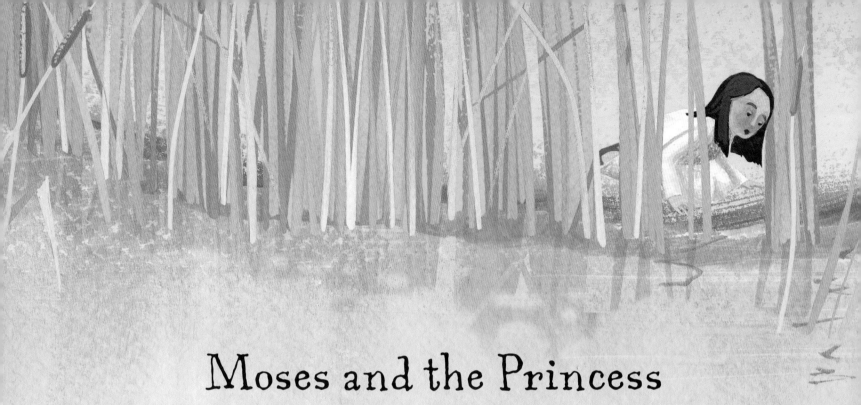

Moses and the Princess

Joseph and his family lived happily in Egypt and, over many years, grew into a great nation called the Hebrews. Long after Joseph died, Egypt had a new Pharaoh, who was a very cruel man. He was afraid that the Hebrews would try to take over his country, so he made them all into slaves.

The Hebrews were made to work hard from very early in the morning until late at night. They built great cities and temples with bricks made of mud and straw. Still the Pharaoh was worried that they would become too powerful, so he ordered his soldiers to kill all the baby Hebrew boys.

One mother hid her baby son from the soldiers to keep
him safe. But she was afraid that the soldiers would hear
him crying and kill him.

Early one morning, she carried the baby down to
the River Nile. There she made a basket of reeds. She put
the sleeping baby gently inside the basket and placed it
among the reeds along the bank.

The baby's mother went home, but his sister Miriam stayed. She hid in the reeds and watched to make sure the baby was safe.

A little later, the Pharaoh's daughter came down to the river to bathe. She was very surprised to see the basket floating on the water. "Bring it to me," she said to one of her servants.

When the princess looked inside the basket, she gasped.
At that moment, the baby woke up and began to cry.
"This must be a Hebrew baby," whispered the princess.
She felt very sorry for him. "I'll keep him," she said,
"so that the soldiers can't kill him."

Miriam ran out from her hiding place. "Would you like a Hebrew mother to look after the baby for you?" she asked eagerly.

The princess looked taken aback. Then she smiled. "Yes," she said. "Bring one to me."

The girl ran to her mother and told her what had happened. Quickly, they hurried back to the river. "Take this baby and look after him," said the princess. "I'll pay you well."

So the mother took care of her own baby. He was safe now, under the princess's protection. When he was old enough, she took him back to her. "He is my son now," said the princess, and she named him Moses.

The Plagues of Egypt

Moses grew up as an Egyptian prince, but he never forgot he was a Hebrew. When he saw an Egyptian beat a Hebrew slave, Moses was so angry that he killed the Egyptian.

Moses knew the Pharaoh would have him put to death for this, so he ran away to the desert. There he began to work as a shepherd. One day, as he was looking after his sheep, he saw a burning bush.

When he went closer, he saw that although there were flames the bush itself wasn't being burned up. Then Moses heard God speak to him.

"Moses, you must go back to Egypt," God told him.
"Ask the Pharaoh to let the Hebrews go. He won't want to,
but I will make him, and everyone will know that I am God.
Then you must bring the Hebrews to me on Mount Sinai
and I will show them the way to a good land."

Moses was frightened, but he knew he must obey God.
He and his brother Aaron went to the Pharaoh and asked
him to free the Hebrews. "No," replied the Pharaoh angrily,
and he made the Hebrew slaves work even harder.

God told Moses to go back to the Pharaoh. This time,
Moses said, "If you won't let the Hebrews go,
terrible things will happen in Egypt."
But again the Pharaoh refused.

Then the terrible things began. First, the water of the River Nile turned into blood. No one could drink it and the fish all died. Soon after that, thousands and thousands of frogs hopped out of the river and into all the Egyptian houses. They were in people's beds, in their ovens and even in their food.

Then tiny gnats crawled out of the dust, and clouds of horrible flies filled the Pharaoh's palace and the houses of the Egyptians. Still the Pharaoh wouldn't let the Hebrews go.

Next, the Egyptians' animals died, and the Egyptian people broke out in horrible sores. Huge hailstones flattened all their crops, and swarms of locusts ate what was left. Then, clouds hid the sun and it was dark for three days. Even after this, the Pharaoh wouldn't free the Hebrews.

The most terrible thing of all was still to come. God warned
Moses about it and told him how to keep the Hebrews safe.
Each Hebrew family killed a lamb and put a little blood on
the doorpost of their house. Then they roasted the lamb and
ate it with flat bread and herbs. That night, the eldest child of
every Egyptian family died, but death passed over the Hebrew
houses. God said the Hebrews should always
remember the night and mark it with
a special festival called the Passover.

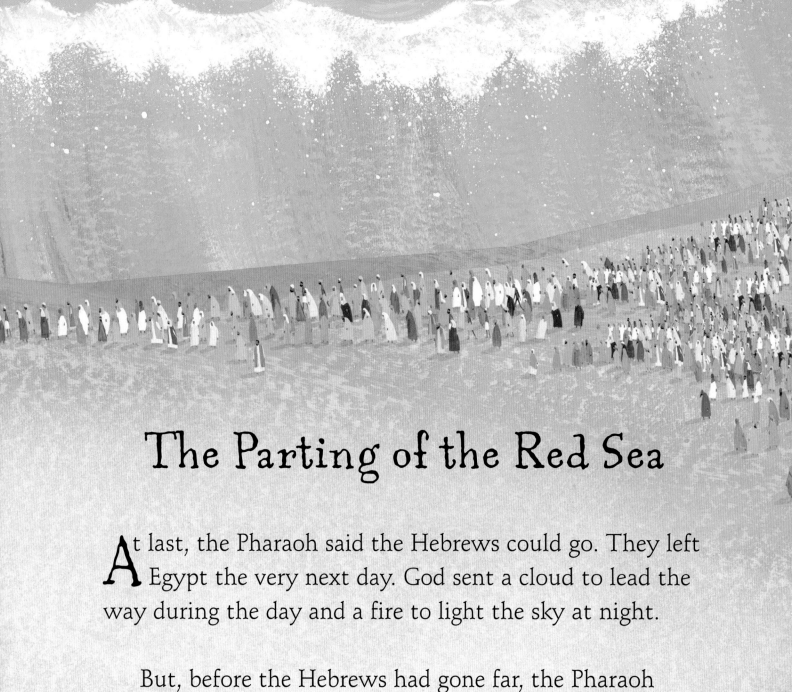

The Parting of the Red Sea

At last, the Pharaoh said the Hebrews could go. They left Egypt the very next day. God sent a cloud to lead the way during the day and a fire to light the sky at night.

But, before the Hebrews had gone far, the Pharaoh changed his mind. He sent his army racing after them in chariots. The Hebrews were terrified. In front of them was the Red Sea and behind them were the Pharaoh's soldiers.

Moses told them not to be afraid. "God will help you," he said. Then he pointed across the water. God sent a great wind. It blew and blew until it drove the sea back, leaving a dry path through the middle. The Hebrews began to hurry across, but the Egyptian soldiers were close behind them.

As soon as the Hebrews reached the other side, Moses raised his hand. At once, the sea rushed in, swallowing up the chariots and drowning all the Egyptian soldiers. The Hebrews were free at last.

Journey through the Desert

Moses led the Hebrews across the desert. They walked for weeks and weeks, and became very tired and hungry. "We should have stayed in Egypt," they grumbled. "There we had plenty to eat. It was better to be slaves than die here in the desert."

God heard them complaining. He said to Moses, "Tell them I will send food for them to eat."

That evening, flocks of small birds called quails landed on their tents. They caught the birds and roasted them to eat. The next morning, the ground was covered with small white flakes. "What's this?" everyone asked.

"Food from God," Moses told them. It was like bread made with honey. They called it manna.

Now people had plenty to eat, but they couldn't find any water to drink. They started to grumble again. "What shall I do?" Moses asked God. "These people are almost ready to kill me."

"Strike that rock with your stick," God told him. When Moses hit the rock, water gushed out in a great stream. There was plenty for everyone.

God looked after the Hebrews during their journey through the desert and made sure they always had enough to eat and drink.

Moses and the Laws of God

At last, Moses and the Hebrews reached Mount Sinai. They set up camp at the foot of the great mountain. Then God told Moses to go to the people and tell them to get ready for him to come to them.

On the morning of the third day, the sky grew dark. There was a deep rumble of thunder, and lightning flashed across the sky.

Everyone rushed out of their tents to see what was happening. The mountain was cloaked in smoke. Flames shot out of it and it shook violently. Then a trumpet blast sounded. It was so loud that they all trembled with fear. They knew that God was near.

Then God called Moses to the top of the mountain and spoke to him. He gave him ten laws that the people must always obey. Moses wrote down these laws on blocks of stone:

I am your God. You must have no other gods but me.
You must not make idols, nor bow down to idols.
When you say my name, you must say it with respect.
Work for six days. Keep the seventh day as a holy day of rest.
Always treat your mother and father with respect.
Do not kill any human being.
Husbands and wives must be faithful to each other.
Do not steal.
Do not tell lies about other people.
Do not envy what other people have.

Joshua and the City of Jericho

When Moses died, a man called Joshua was chosen to lead the Hebrews to the land that God had promised them. It was on the other side of the River Jordan. The water was very high, but God helped them across. They were there at last.

The first place they came to was a city called Jericho. But the great wooden gates were closed and the people wouldn't let them in. Joshua gazed up at the huge stone walls. "How can we get into the city?" he wondered. Then God told him what to do.

Every day for six days, Joshua marched the people around the city walls. Seven priests blew trumpets, but no one else made a sound. On the seventh day, they marched around the city seven times. Then the priests blew their trumpets.

"God has given us the city," cried Joshua, and everyone shouted as loudly as they could. Suddenly, there was a great crash as the huge walls tumbled to the ground. Everyone rushed into the city. It was theirs. With God's help they had won their first battle.

The people settled in the promised land, and grew into a strong nation, called the Israelites.

The Mighty Samson

After many years, the Israelites forgot to obey God's laws. Their enemies, the Philistines, attacked them and ruled over them. Then God sent some people to help the Israelites. One of these helpers was called Samson.

Before Samson was born, an angel had told his mother never to cut his hair, to show that he belonged to God. She didn't, and it grew longer and longer, until it flowed down to his waist.

As Samson's hair grew, so did his strength. Once, he was out walking when a lion ran at him, roaring loudly. Samson grabbed the lion and killed it with his bare hands. He knew that it was God who made him so strong.

Samson fought the Philistines whenever he could. He set fire to their crops and killed them in battles. Then he fell in love with a beautiful Philistine girl, called Delilah. The Philistines promised to make her rich if she could find out why Samson was so strong.

Delilah begged Samson to tell her his secret, but he just made up lots of stories. "If you really loved me," said Delilah, "you would tell me the truth."

Again and again she asked Samson, until at last he gave in. "My long hair shows that I belong to God," he said. "Without it, I would be no stronger than anyone else."

That night, when Samson was fast asleep, Delilah let in a man to cut off Samson's hair.

When Samson woke up, his strength had gone. The Philistines captured him easily. They blinded him and threw him into prison. Slowly, Samson's hair began to grow again, but the Philistines didn't notice.

One day, the Philistines held a great feast in their temple to praise their god Dagon for helping them to capture Samson. They led Samson to the temple and made him stand between two huge pillars that held up the temple roof.

Samson put his hands on the pillars and asked
God to make him strong again. Then he pushed with
all his might. With a deafening crash, the roof fell in
on top of them. The Philistine rulers were killed, along
with thousands of others. Samson died too, but he
had brought peace to the Israelites and it was many
years before the Philistines threatened them again.

David and Goliath

David was only a boy, but he was strong and brave.
He looked after his father's sheep out on the hills all
by himself. To pass the time, he would often play his little
harp. Sometimes, he had to fight off bears and wolves
that wanted to eat the sheep and lambs. He fired stones
at them with his sling.

One day, David's father asked him to take some food to his brothers. They were soldiers in King Saul's army. The army was camped on one side of a valley and on the other side were their enemies, the Philistines.

Among the Philistines was a soldier called Goliath, who was a giant of a man. "Who dares to come and fight me?" he shouted across the valley.

King Saul's soldiers were all too scared, but David was not afraid. "I'll fight him," he said.

"But you're just a child," said King Saul.

"I have killed bears and wolves, with God's help,"
said David. "He will help me now."

King Saul wanted David to take his sword and shield,
but they were too heavy for him. Instead, David picked up
five stones for his sling.

When Goliath saw David striding over with his sling,
he burst out laughing. "They've sent a child to fight me!"
he exclaimed. "I'll soon finish him off."

"You may have a sword and a spear,
but I've got God on my side,"
shouted David.

David put a stone in his sling and swung it around his head, faster and faster. Then he let it go. The stone hurtled through the air and hit Goliath in the middle of his forehead. He fell to the ground with a crash. The giant was dead.

When the Philistine army saw this, they all ran away in terror. King Saul's army chased them, right up to the walls of their city. With God's help, David had won the battle for them.

Jonah's Journey

One day, God spoke to a man named Jonah. "I want you to go to the city of Nineveh," he said. "Tell the people that they are very bad and they must change their ways."

Jonah didn't want to go to Nineveh. Instead, he ran to the port and found a ship going the other way. He hid in the bottom of the boat, where he thought God wouldn't be able to find him.

Soon after the ship set sail, a terrible storm blew up. Huge waves tossed the ship about. The sailors were terrified. They thought the ship would sink and they would all drown. Everyone began to pray.

The captain found Jonah fast asleep. He shook him hard. "How can you sleep through this?" he shouted above the noise of the wind. "Get up. You must pray too."

"I can't pray to God. I'm running away from him," Jonah yelled back.

The sailors thought the storm was Jonah's fault. "Tell us how to make it go away," they begged.

"You must throw me into the sea," said Jonah. The sailors didn't want Jonah to drown, but the storm was so bad that, at last, they picked him up and dropped him into the water. At once, the sea became calm again.

Jonah sank down and down in the water. Just as he thought he would drown, an enormous fish swam up and swallowed him whole.

"God has sent this fish to save me," thought Jonah. He lived inside it for three whole days and nights. Then the great fish swam to the shore and spat Jonah out onto dry land, safe and sound.

"Now you must go to Nineveh," said God, and this time Jonah did as he was told. He warned the people of Nineveh that unless they gave up their bad ways and obeyed the laws of God, God would destroy their city in forty days' time.

The king of Nineveh ordered his people to tell God they were sorry and would obey his laws. When God saw that they had changed, he didn't want to hurt them.

Jonah sat outside the city and waited. He was feeling hot and fed up. He wanted God to punish the people of Nineveh. "Jonah," said God, "I love everyone and it is right that I should forgive them, for they are sorry for the bad things they have done."

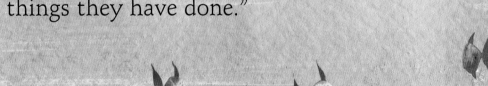

Daniel and the Lions

Daniel was just a boy when his city, Jerusalem, was captured by an enemy army. The army had been sent by God because the Israelites kept on disobeying him. Daniel and thousands of other people were taken to Babylon.

Daniel was picked out to serve in the king's palace. His enemies were kind to him. They sent him to a good school, fed him well and looked after him. But Daniel always remembered to say his prayers to God.

Daniel grew up to be a wise and clever man. He was so wise that the king decided to make him one of his three rulers, who looked after the kingdom for him.

The other two rulers were jealous of Daniel. They watched him all the time to try to catch him doing something wrong, but Daniel was always honest and true. "We must find a way to get rid of him," they said.

The two rulers went to the king. "King Darius, please make a new law," they said. "For thirty days, everyone must pray only to you, or they'll be fed to the lions." King Darius agreed to make the law.

Daniel heard about the new law, but he still prayed to God three times a day. When the rulers saw him, they went to tell the king. "Daniel's broken your law," they said. "He must die."

King Darius was upset, because he liked and trusted Daniel. He tried to think of a way to save him, but Daniel had broken the law and he had to be punished.

With a heavy heart, the king ordered Daniel to be thrown into a pit with hungry lions. "May your God save you," he said to him.

Very early the next morning, the king hurried to the lion pit. "Did your God save you?" he shouted to Daniel.

"Yes," Daniel shouted back. "God wouldn't let the lions hurt me. He knows I've done nothing wrong."

The king was delighted that Daniel was safe. "Set him free at once," he ordered the guards, "and put the other two rulers in with the lions."

Then King Darius made a new law. Everyone in his kingdom was to respect Daniel's God, the God who had saved Daniel from the lions.

The New Testament

The New Testament

Mary and the Angel

Mary lived in the village of Nazareth. Soon, she was going to marry Joseph, who was a carpenter in the village. One day, when she was alone, an angel appeared in front of her. She was very scared.

"Don't be afraid, Mary," said the angel. "I am Gabriel. God has sent me to tell you that you are going to have a son. You must name him Jesus. He will be a great king and his kingdom will last forever."

Mary stared at the angel. She was puzzled. "There must be some mistake," she said. "I'm not married yet. How can I have a baby?"

"There's no mistake," said Gabriel. "Your son will be the son of God."

Mary bowed her head and thought about what Gabriel had told her. "I'll do whatever God wants," she said at last. When she looked up, Gabriel had gone.

Joseph was a good, kind man, but when he heard that Mary was expecting a baby, he was shocked. He thought he shouldn't marry her.

That night, Joseph had a dream. In it, an angel said to him, "You should marry Mary. She will have a child who is the son of God. You are to name him Jesus. He will save people from God's punishment for all the bad things they've done."

When Joseph woke up, he remembered his dream. He did what the angel had told him to do and married Mary.

Jesus is Born

Mary and Joseph lived happily in Nazareth, waiting for Mary's son to be born. Then the Roman rulers of the country made a new law. Everyone had to go to their family's home town to register their names for taxes.

Mary and Joseph had to go to a place called Bethlehem. By the time they arrived, it was getting dark. Mary was very, very tired. It was nearly time for her to have her baby.

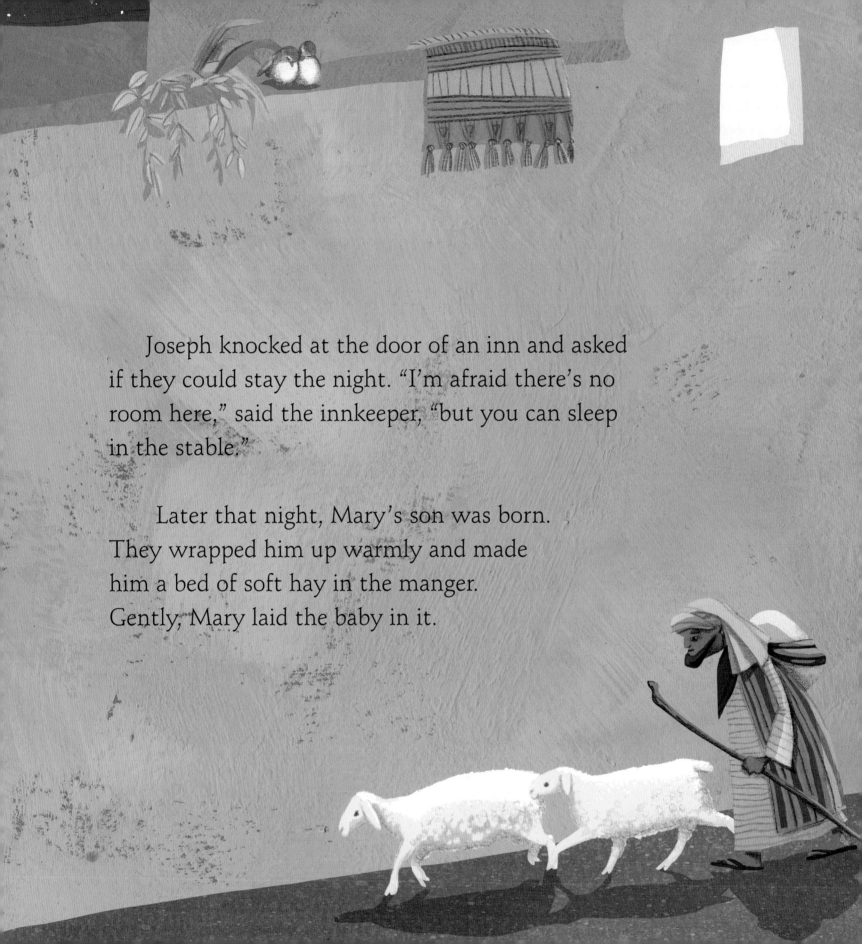

Joseph knocked at the door of an inn and asked
if they could stay the night. "I'm afraid there's no
room here," said the innkeeper, "but you can sleep
in the stable."

Later that night, Mary's son was born.
They wrapped him up warmly and made
him a bed of soft hay in the manger.
Gently, Mary laid the baby in it.

The Shepherds

In the fields outside Bethlehem, some shepherds were watching over their sheep. Suddenly, there was a dazzling light and an angel stood in front of them. The shepherds shrank back in terror.

"Don't be frightened," said the angel. "I bring you wonderful news. Tonight the son of God was born in a stable in Bethlehem. You will find him lying in a manger."

All at once the sky was filled with angels, singing,
"Glory to God in the highest and peace to those he loves."
The shepherds gazed open-mouthed at the glorious sight.

Then, as suddenly as they came, the angels disappeared,
and the night was dark again. "We must go to Bethlehem,"
said one of the shepherds quietly. They packed up their
things and went to look for the stable.

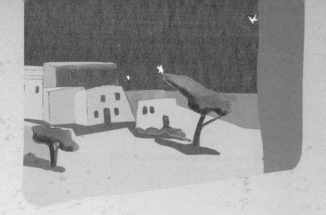

When the shepherds found the stable, they crept inside and tiptoed over to the manger to see the baby. They told Mary and Joseph what the angel had said to them.

Then the shepherds rushed off to tell everyone the good news that the son of God had been born in a stable that night. Everyone was amazed at what they heard.

The Wise Men

F ar away from Bethlehem, some wise men saw a shining new star in the night sky. They knew it meant something special had happened. "A child has been born who will be king of the Jews," said one.

The wise men agreed they must go and find him.
They began their long journey, taking presents with them
for the new king.

At last, the wise men came to the city of Jerusalem.
"Where can we find the baby who is born king of the
Jews?" they asked.

When King Herod heard who the strangers were
looking for, he was worried. He was already king of
the Jews and he didn't want someone else taking over.
He called his priests and asked them about the baby.
They said he could be found in Bethlehem.

King Herod had a secret meeting with the wise men. "I would like to see this baby too," he told them. "Come back when you have found him and tell me where he is."

The wise men left Jerusalem and followed the star all the way to Bethlehem. When it came to the place where Jesus lay, the star came to a stop.

They went inside and knelt down beside the baby. They gave him presents of gold, sweet-smelling frankincense and a special ointment called myrrh. Then they crept quietly away.

That night, the wise men had a dream. In it, an angel said to them, "Don't go back to Jerusalem. King Herod wants to kill the baby Jesus." The wise men didn't want any harm to come to Jesus, so the next morning they decided not to go back to Jerusalem, but to take a different way home.

Joseph had a dream too. "Jesus is in great danger,"
an angel told him. "You must take him and Mary to Egypt."
Joseph woke Mary and told her they
must leave at once. Quickly, they
packed up their things and hurried
away into the dark night.

King Herod waited and waited, but there was no sign of the wise men. When he realized that they weren't coming back, he was beside himself with rage.

He stormed up and down, shouting and waving his fists. He wasn't going to wait for this new baby king to grow up and seize his throne.

King Herod made a plan to get rid of the baby. He ordered his soldiers to march to Bethlehem and kill all the baby boys who were under two years old.

But Mary, Joseph and Jesus were already living safely in Egypt, where King Herod couldn't hurt them.

Some time later, Joseph had another dream. An angel said to him, "Joseph, King Herod is dead. It is safe for you to go home now."

Then Joseph took Mary and Jesus back to Nazareth, where they settled down happily in their own house.

Jesus in the Temple

Jesus grew up in Nazareth. He went to school and learned the laws of God. When he was twelve years old, Mary and Joseph took him to Jerusalem for the feast of the Passover. This feast reminded the Jews that God had freed them from slavery in Egypt all those years ago.

When it was all over, Mary and Joseph joined lots of other families going back to Nazareth. They thought Jesus was walking with some other boys. It wasn't until they camped for the night that they realized he was missing.

Mary and Joseph hunted high and low for him. "Have you seen Jesus?" they asked first one person, and then another. But no one had seen him that evening. They grew more and more worried.

The next morning, Mary and Joseph hurried back to Jerusalem. For three days, they searched for Jesus. At last, they found him in the temple, sitting with the temple teachers. He was listening to them and asking questions. Everyone was very surprised at how much he knew and understood.

"Where have you been? We were so worried," cried Mary. "We've searched everywhere. We thought we'd lost you."

Jesus looked surprised. "I'm sorry," he said, getting up. "I didn't mean to worry you. But why were you looking for me? Didn't you know I'd be here in my Father's house?"

Then Jesus went back home to Nazareth with Mary and Joseph, and he was obedient to them.

John the Baptist

own by the River Jordan, Jesus' cousin John was telling
people all about God. Everyone crowded around to listen.
"You must stop being so greedy," he told them. "Share your
food with people who are hungry and give your spare clothes
to people who don't have any."

John used water from the river to baptize the people.
They knew they had done bad things, but this washing in
the river showed they could make a new start.

John told them that soon someone much more
important would be coming. "I am not worthy to
undo his sandals," he said. He was talking about Jesus.

Then, one day, Jesus came and asked John to baptize
him too. "But you should baptize me," said John.

"Let us do what God wants," replied Jesus. He waded
into the river and John dipped him in the water.

As Jesus stepped out of the river, a white dove flew
down from the sky and hovered above him. Then he heard
God's voice saying, "You are my dear son and I am very
pleased with you."

Jesus and his Friends

Jesus lived in Nazareth until he was about thirty years old. Then he went to live near Lake Galilee. There he taught people about God and made those who were ill well again. Soon, large crowds gathered to listen to him.

One day, when Jesus was walking beside the lake, he saw two fishermen, called Peter and Andrew. He climbed into their boat and asked them to row out onto the lake. "Now put out your fishing nets," he said.

"We've fished all night long and caught nothing," said Peter, "but if you say so we will do it." Then they lowered the nets into the water.

Soon, the nets were so full of fish that they almost broke. Peter and Andrew shouted over to two other fishermen, James and John, to help them. Together they filled both boats with fish.

When the four men saw how many fish Jesus had helped them to catch, they were alarmed. "Don't be frightened," said Jesus. "Come with me. From now on you will catch people instead of fish. I want you to bring the people to me." So Peter and Andrew, James and John left their boats and went with Jesus.

Jesus asked a man called Matthew to come with him too. Nobody liked Matthew. He collected taxes for the hated Roman rulers.

When some religious people saw Jesus having a meal with Matthew and some of his friends, they asked each other, "Why does such a good man eat with bad people?"

Jesus overheard them. "The people who are good don't need me," he explained. "I've come to ask bad people to change their ways."

One evening, Jesus walked up a mountain and stayed there all night, praying to God. The next day, he chose some more friends. They were Philip, Bartholomew, Thomas, another James, Simon, Judas and Judas Iscariot. That made twelve in all. They were called his disciples. They went everywhere with Jesus. He taught them about God and they saw the wonderful things he did.

A Special Prayer

Wherever Jesus went with his disciples, crowds of people came to listen to him. As the weather was hot and dry, he often talked to them outside.

"Riches will not make you happy," Jesus told them. "You should be content with what you already have. God knows what you need and he will look after you. He takes care of the poor. The kingdom of heaven belongs to them."

"It's easy to love your friends," he said, "but you should love everyone, even those people who are horrible to you. If someone does something bad or wrong, be kind to them in return."

"When you do someone a good turn, don't do it to show off to them. Keep it a secret. God sees what you do and will reward you."

"When you say a prayer, say it quietly when you are on your own. Talk to God as you would to a father who loves you. Keep your prayers simple."

Then Jesus said, "Say this prayer when you talk to God:

Our Father who is in heaven,
holy is your name.
May your kingdom come.
May your will be done on earth as it is in heaven.

Give us our food each day.
Forgive us the wrongs we have done,
as we forgive the wrongs others have done to us.
Don't let us be tempted to do wrong,
but save us from evil."

A Storm on the Lake

One evening, Jesus asked some of his disciples to take him in a boat across Lake Galilee. There was just a gentle wind blowing as they pushed the boat out onto the water.

Jesus was very tired. When they had gone a little way, he lay down in the bottom of the boat and soon he was fast asleep.

The wind blew stronger and stronger. It howled all around them and huge waves crashed over the sides of the little boat. The disciples were afraid that the boat would fill with water and sink.

All through the noise of the wind and the waves, Jesus slept quietly on. At last, one of the men woke him up. "Master," he shouted, "can't you see that we're all going to drown?"

Jesus stood up and looked around. "Hush, be still," he said. At once, the wind dropped and the water was calm. "You shouldn't be so afraid," he told the disciples.

The disciples were amazed. "Who is this man who can even tell the wind and waves what to do?" they whispered to each other nervously.

The boat sailed on, and Jesus and his disciples landed safely on the shore of the lake.

Jesus and the Little Girl

When Jesus was walking through a town one day, a man called Jairus ran up to him. He knelt down on the ground in front of Jesus. "My little daughter is very ill," he said in despair. "I think she is dying. Please come to my house and make her better."

Jesus and some of his disciples went to the house, but before they got there, they saw someone coming out crying. "It's too late, Jairus. Your little girl is dead," he said. "There's no point bringing Jesus now."

Jesus went into the house with Peter, James and John. "She's not dead. She's asleep," he said. Then he made everyone leave the house except for the disciples and the girl's mother and father.

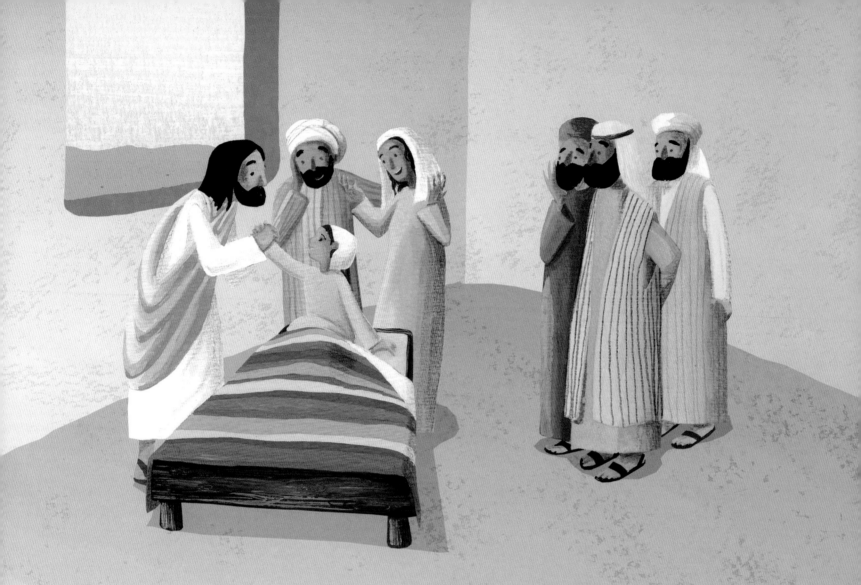

Jesus took hold of the girl's hand. "Little girl, get up,"
he said. At once, she opened her eyes and sat up, smiling.
Her mother and father wept with joy. They were astonished
to see her alive and well.

"Give her some food," said Jesus gently, "and tell no one
about this." Then he and his disciples quietly left the house.

The Loaves and the Fishes

One day, Jesus and his disciples sailed across Lake Galilee to a place on the opposite shore. Jesus wanted to have a little time on his own.

But some people spotted the boat and followed it, walking along the shore of the lake. More and more people came, until there was a great crowd.

The disciples wanted to send the people away, but Jesus felt sorry for them. He walked among them, talked to them and made those who were ill well again.

As the sun began to go down, one of the disciples said to Jesus, "We should send these people home. They are hungry and there's nothing here for them to eat."

"No," said Jesus. "If they are hungry, we must give them something to eat."

"There's nowhere to buy food," muttered Philip, "and even if there were, it would cost a huge amount of money to buy enough for all of them."

Andrew brought a young boy to Jesus. "This boy has five small loaves and two fishes," he said, "but that won't go far among all these people."

Jesus looked down at the boy and smiled. "May I take your food?" he asked.

"Yes, Master," said the boy.

"Tell the people to sit down," Jesus said to the disciples. The disciples walked among the people, asking them to sit on the grass. There were more than five thousand men, women and children.

Jesus held up the boy's five small loaves and two fishes, and said a prayer to God. Then he broke up the bread and fishes and handed them to the disciples. "Give this food out to the people," he said.

The more food the disciples gave out, the more there was. They were very, very puzzled.

There was more than enough food to feed everyone. The people ate as much as they wanted and when they had finished they went happily back to their homes.

"Collect up all the leftover food," Jesus said to the disciples. "Nothing must be wasted."

The disciples wandered over the hillside, picking up the food. They filled twelve whole baskets with the leftovers.

The Good Samaritan

One day, Jesus was talking to a crowd
of people when a clever lawyer said
to him, "I know I should be kind to
other people, but which people?"
Then Jesus told him this story.

A Jew left his home in Jerusalem to walk
to Jericho. It was a long, lonely road. When he
was about halfway there, some robbers jumped
out at him. They knocked him down, hit him
and kicked him. Then they stole everything
he had and left him lying on the road.
He was very badly hurt.

After a while, a priest came along on his donkey. He saw the man lying in the dust, but he passed by on the other side of the road.

Later, a man who worked at the temple in Jerusalem walked along the road. He looked at the wounded man, but hurried on his way.

Then a Samaritan came riding by. The Samaritan people had always hated the Jews, but when he saw the man lying on the road, he felt sorry for him.

The Samaritan got off his donkey, knelt down in the dust and bandaged the man's wounds. Then he helped him onto the donkey and led it down the road to an inn. There he gave him some supper and put him to bed.

In the morning, the Samaritan paid the innkeeper.
"Look after this man for me," he said. "Next time I come
I'll pay you anything I owe you."

When Jesus had finished the story, he asked the lawyer,
"Which of these three men was kind?"

"The Samaritan," said the lawyer.

"That's the answer to your question," said Jesus.
"Be like the Samaritan. Be kind to everyone. Not just
your family and friends, but everyone."

The Good Shepherd

Jesus often told people stories to teach them more about God. One day, he said, "If a shepherd has a hundred sheep and one gets lost, what does he do? He leaves the ninety-nine sheep in a safe place and goes to look for the one missing sheep."

"The shepherd looks everywhere for that one sheep, listening hard to hear it bleating. He doesn't care how long it takes. He won't give up until he has found the sheep. Then he picks it up, puts it on his shoulders and carries it home. He calls his family and friends to celebrate with him that he has found his one lost sheep."

"There is joy like that in heaven when just one person in trouble comes back to God," said Jesus. "I am like the good shepherd. I look after my people. I never run away and leave them when they're in danger. Like the sheep, they know my voice and follow me. I lead and protect them and I am ready to die for them."

The Wasteful Son

Jesus said to the people, "When someone is sorry for their bad ways and wants to please God, there is joy in heaven." Then he told them this story.

A rich farmer had two sons. The younger son came to him and said, "Father, half of what you have will be mine one day. Give it to me now." The father was very unhappy, but he gave his son what he asked for.

The son went to live in a city far away. He bought new clothes and a big house with lots of servants. Every evening, he gave feasts for his new, rich friends.

Soon, he had spent all his money and had to sell everything. He got a job looking after a man's pigs. Sometimes, he was so hungry he felt like eating the pigs' food.

In the end, he decided to go home. When his father saw him coming, he ran to meet him. The son hung his head.
"Forgive me," he said. "I don't deserve to be your son."

"Of course I forgive you," cried his father. He told his servants to bring new clothes and shoes for his son. Then he arranged a special dinner and invited all their friends.

The other son was angry. He complained that his father had never given him anything. "You are my son and I love you," said his father. "Please try to understand. I thought your brother was lost or dead, and I'm so happy he has come home alive and well."

Jesus Rides to Jerusalem

Jesus and his disciples were going to Jerusalem. They wanted to be there for the festival of the Passover. On the way, they stopped at a village. Two of the disciples borrowed a donkey. They spread their cloaks over it and Jesus got on. Then, with his disciples at his side, he rode into Jerusalem.

Crowds of people came out to meet Jesus. They were very excited. Some spread their cloaks on the ground. Others cut down palm leaves and laid them in front of the donkey. They cheered and shouted, "Blessed is he who comes in the name of the Lord. Praise be to God."

Jesus and his disciples went to the temple to pray. It was like a busy market. There were people buying and selling cows, sheep and pigeons, and changing money.

Jesus was very angry. "God's house is a house of prayer," he shouted, "but you have turned it into a den of robbers." Then he overturned their tables and drove them away.

When the temple rulers heard what Jesus had done, they decided to get rid of him. Judas Iscariot, one of the disciples, slipped away to meet them. "I can tell you when would be a good time to arrest Jesus," he said, "but what will you give me?"

"We will give you thirty silver coins," they said. From then on, Judas watched and waited for the right moment.

The Last Supper

On the morning of the feast of the Passover, the disciples came to Jesus and asked him where they could have their special meal.

"Go to Jerusalem," Jesus said to Peter and John. "You will see a man carrying a jar of water. Follow him to his house. We will have our meal there in a room upstairs."

Peter and John did as Jesus told them. They found the house and made the room ready for the meal. In the evening, Jesus and the other disciples joined them.

As Jesus sat down at the table, his disciples could see that something was wrong. He looked so sad.

Jesus knew he wouldn't be with them for much longer, and that he would die soon. "Before the night is over, one of you is going to betray me," he said to them.

The disciples were horrified. They looked at each other in silence, wondering who it could be.

"It's the one I give this bread to," said Jesus. He broke off a piece of bread and handed it to Judas Iscariot. "Do what you have to do," he said.

Judas got up from the table and hurried away into the night. When he had gone, Jesus told the disciples how much he loved them. He said that he was going to die, but they wouldn't be alone. God would send his Holy Spirit to help them.

Jesus picked up a loaf of bread and said a prayer
to God. "Eat this bread and remember me," he said, and
handed a piece to each disciple. Then he picked up a cup
of wine and gave thanks to God. "Drink this wine and
remember me," he said.

When Jesus and his disciples had finished the supper, they walked to a place called the Garden of Gethsemane. On the way, Jesus told his disciples that soon they would all run away and leave him. "I would never do that," said Peter.

In the garden, Jesus walked away from his disciples to pray on his own. When he came back, they were asleep. Jesus woke them quietly. Just then, they heard voices and saw flaming torches through the trees.

Judas was leading the chief priests and
temple guards to them. He walked up to Jesus
and kissed him on the cheek. "This is the man
you want," he said.

Peter drew his sword, but Jesus made him put it away. When the temple guards grabbed hold of Jesus, the disciples were afraid. They all ran away, even Peter, just as Jesus had said they would. Then the guards marched Jesus back to Jerusalem.

Death on a Cross

The guards led Jesus to the palace of Caiaphas, the high priest. All night long, the chief priests and Jewish leaders asked Jesus questions, but he didn't answer them. Many people told lies about him.

The leaders tried to find a reason to have Jesus killed, but he had done nothing wrong. At last, the high priest asked him, "Are you the son of God?"

"I am," Jesus answered.

"You heard what he said," the high priest shouted excitedly. "We don't need any more witnesses. He claims to be the son of God. You heard it from his own lips. Is he guilty or not guilty?"

"Guilty," shouted the others. "Kill him." They hit Jesus and spat at him.

When Judas heard that Jesus was going to be killed, he was terribly sorry he'd betrayed him. He went to the temple and threw down the thirty silver coins they had given him. Then he went out and hanged himself.

In the morning, Jesus was taken to Pontius Pilate, the Roman governor. He soon realized that Jesus had done nothing wrong and he wanted to let him go.

Pilate offered to set one prisoner free, but the people chose a very bad man named Barabbas instead. "What shall I do with Jesus?" asked Pilate.

"Crucify him, crucify him," they shouted.

Pilate didn't want to be blamed for Jesus' death, but he was afraid he would get into trouble. In the end, he gave the order that Jesus was to die.

The guards led Jesus away. They dressed him in a purple robe, placed a crown of thorns upon his head and put a stick in his hand. Then they knelt in front of him, laughing and jeering. "Hail, king of the Jews," they shouted, and they beat him.

Afterwards, the guards dressed Jesus in his own clothes again. They made him carry a heavy wooden cross through the streets of Jerusalem. Tired and weak from their beatings, Jesus stumbled and fell, again and again.

They led Jesus to a place called Golgotha. The guards nailed his hands and feet to the cross, and they put a sign over his head that said, "Jesus of Nazareth. King of the Jews." Then they set up the cross between two other crosses. On these crosses there were two thieves.

People crowded around the crosses. Among them was Mary, Jesus' mother. With her was John, one of the disciples. Jesus looked down at them. "Take care of her as a son would," he said to John.

At noon, the sky grew strangely dark. The people silently watched and waited. At three o'clock, Jesus looked up and cried out, "Father, into your hands I give my spirit." Then he bowed his head and died.

The ground started to shake. Many of the soldiers and people were afraid. One soldier looked up at Jesus and said, "This man really was the son of God."

The soldiers took Jesus down from the cross. Some of his friends carried him to a tomb outside Jerusalem. They laid his body in the tomb and rolled a heavy stone in front of it. Then they went quietly away. It was now Friday evening.

The Empty Tomb

Early on Sunday morning, Jesus' friend Mary Magdalene went to his tomb with some other women. They were shocked to see the heavy stone in front of it had been rolled away. An angel dressed in snow-white robes was standing beside it. "Jesus is not here," he told them. "He is alive."

When they looked into the tomb, they saw it was empty. Feeling confused and frightened, they ran to tell Peter and John.

Peter and John hurried to the tomb and saw that it was true. Jesus really was gone. They were both amazed.

Mary Magdalene went back to the tomb on her own and knelt down outside it. "Mary," said a voice beside her, "go and tell my friends you have seen me and that soon I'll be with God in heaven."

Mary looked up and saw that it was Jesus. Full of joy, she ran to the disciples. "I've seen Jesus and he spoke to me," she cried.

On the Road to Emmaus

Later that evening, two of Jesus' friends were walking from Jerusalem to the village of Emmaus. Jesus came up and walked with them, but they thought he was a stranger. "Why are you so sad?" Jesus asked them.

"We were talking about Jesus," said one. "We thought he was sent by God to save our people, but the chief priests and Roman rulers have killed him."

When they reached Emmaus, the two men asked the stranger to have supper with them. He said a prayer, broke some bread into pieces and gave it to them. They knew at once that the stranger was Jesus. They stared at him for a moment, and then he was gone.

The two men ran back to Jerusalem and told the disciples that they had spoken to Jesus. Suddenly, Jesus was in the room with them. At first, they were scared, but Jesus said, "Don't be afraid. Look at the wounds on my hands and feet. Touch me and feel that I am real."

Then they knew it really was Jesus. He told them that this was part of God's plan. "I had to die and then come alive again on the third day," he said. "God forgives everyone who believes in me. This is the message for all the people in the world, and you must go and tell them."

Breakfast by the Lake

One evening, Peter and some of the disciples sailed in a boat across Lake Galilee. They fished all night, but caught nothing. In the morning, they saw a man standing on the shore. They didn't know it was Jesus. "Have you caught any fish?" he called.

"No, nothing," they called back.

"Throw your net over the right side of the boat," he said. They dropped the net in the water, and soon it was so full of fish that they couldn't pull it up.

One of the disciples said, "It must be Jesus." When Peter heard this, he jumped into the water and swam to the shore. The others rowed the boat to the beach and dragged in the net.

Jesus lit a fire and cooked some of the fish over it. "Come and have breakfast," he said to the disciples. When they had finished, he turned to Peter. "Take good care of my people," he said.

Wind and Fire

Jesus was walking with his disciples on the Mount of Olives, outside Jerusalem. The time had come for him to say goodbye.

"Go back to Jerusalem," Jesus told them. "Very soon God will send you his Holy Spirit. He will give you the power to speak bravely about me and all that I have taught you. You will speak to the people in Jerusalem and all over the whole world."

When Jesus had finished, he was taken up into heaven before their eyes. Then a cloud hid him from them. The disciples looked up and saw two men dressed in white. "Jesus has gone to be with God," they said, "but one day he will come back."

The disciples went back to Jerusalem. One day, they were all together to celebrate a Jewish festival.

Suddenly, they heard a noise like a great wind blowing through the room. Then fire flickered around their heads, but the flames didn't burn them. At that moment, they all began to speak in different languages.

They knew this was a sign that God had given them the power to speak bravely to the people. The disciples rushed out into the streets and told everyone they met about Jesus and the wonderful things he had done.

With thanks to
Georgina Andrews, James Brown
and Alex Frith for their advice.

Digital manipulation by Mike Wheatley
and John Russell.